Dragon Tears

By

Nichole Haggerty

This book is a work of fiction. Places, events, and situations in this story are purely fictional. Any resemblance to actual persons, living or dead, is coincidental.

ISBN: 1-4107-6356-0 (e-book)
ISBN: 1-4107-6357-9 (Paperback)

Library of Congress Control Number: 2003093902

This book is printed on acid free paper.

Printed in the United States of America
Bloomington, IN

1stBooks – rev. 7/16/03

A silent poet
Speaks true words
A blind poet
Sees the truth
A poet with no face
Will be heard

Can it be true?
Is there no reality?
Only deception
Maybe its paranoia
It could just be the drink
It could just be the drugs
Make it go away
I don't want to stay
Would you cry?
If I were to bleed
Would you care?
Destruction and chaos
Overwhelm me
Flood my mind
And cause my soul to perish
No apology necessary
I live in the hell you created
If I could live
You would die
So you'll kill me first
And I'll just smile
While you cry

It's wet outside
It's cold inside
Screeching tires
Shattering glass
No one with a heart
No one with courage
Hold me close
I'm losing my breath
Life brought to an abrupt stop
Maybe I would have been something
Maybe people would have known me
I could have had a house
I could have had children
I could have had love
I'll never know
You'll forget except once a year

My heart and head
Working against each other
Society on the streets
Break free go home
Fly away from my soul
Indulge my body
Forget about my life
So much to do
Break free from my chains
Loving pillows
Strangling sheets

In the middle of life
Out of love
Full of hate
A part of society
Behind the walls
Under the streets
Leaking through the cracks
We're finding our way through
We're finding our way in
Hide your face
Show your fear
Go ahead and run
We'll just walk
I can feel you
These are the eyes of the blind
This is the heart of the heartless
Your breaths of vanity
Your feet of lies
Kill your soul
Make the children cry
We're coming out
This is the voice of truth

Can you hear me, or did you forget me
Standing in the rain
Your eyes are cold
Full of death
My mind imprisoned in your hatred
Ignorance chains me to the wall
My body so cold
So lifeless
Drain me of my will
Of my freedom
Another lost soul
Add to your collection
A tear to remember
Two to forget
The pain fades away
The anger never stops growing

Maybe one-day things will make sense
Maybe they won't
Smile and forget about the pain
Go on one won't hurt
Don't think about the bottom
You can always get another one
Smile and forget about the pain
Go ahead two just makes it better
If you're thirsty go ahead and have another drink
After awhile the taste goes numb
Don't think about the bottom we have more
No one has to know
The bottle doesn't gossip
Smile and forget about the pain
Go ahead three won't kill you
Don't doubt the people who are here for you now
Have another drink
Go ahead four will make you forget everything

Nichole Haggerty

Close your eyes
You don't want to see
Your daughter sells herself for a hit
Your son kills to make the team
Death on our streets
Death in our homes
Close your eyes
You don't want to see
Serial killers make their rounds
Take another hit
Lick another stamp
You've been marked
Just another day in your head
Just another reason to run away
You've seen it happen
You've been marked
The doctor turns away
The cops lock you away
There's no way out
You've been marked
So much pain
So much hatred
No more tears
No more years
Killing to stay alive

In this hour of another day
In this day of another week
Nothing changes
It's always the same
Bleeding hands turn into bleeding thoughts
Losing my reason
Losing my faith
My mind decaying
A prisoner of society
Where is my life?
I can't take another day

Nichole Haggerty

Can you feel the pain you put me through?
I know you said you cared
I know you have other plans
Although I can't help but think of you
Maybe with time the feelings will fade away
Perhaps with time the memories will die
Until then it's so hard to say goodbye

It's all the little things I remember
It's all the little things you do that make me smile
When I think of you
It's all the haunting memories fading away
When you hold me
It's all the hateful words without a voice
When you smile
It's all my anger losing life
When you kiss me
It's everything you do that pulls me out of my hell
Through your eyes I learned to forgive
Through my eyes you understood

I'll never forget
You'll never remember
Pin me against the wall
Spit on my soul
Don't hold back
I'll never forget
You'll never remember
Speak your convictions
Stab my mind
Rape me of my feelings
I'll never forget
You'll never remember
Poison your blood
While I watch mine spill
Bruises fade away
Scars never fade
I'll never forget
You'll never remember

Let the streets crumble away
Turn out the lights
Give you my heart and you'll break it
Give you my soul and you'll crush it
Give you my mind and you'll poison it
Let the world turn
Let society keep its ignorance
Give me a gun and I'll kill you
Give me a knife and I'll stab myself
You think I'm insane
I think your blind
Give me my mind and I'll think
Give me my soul and I'll fly
Give me my heart and I'll love
You think I'm depressed
I think you're a fool
Give me my life and I'll live

I think I might be going insane
Maybe it's not in my head
Maybe it's in my heart
Society is strangling me
I'm fighting the inevitable
Losing strength to hold on
My soul will perish
My mind will rot
Their convictions stab me
While their thoughts rape me

I could walk for days
I could look all over the world
But I would never find what makes you happy
It lies within you
Although it's so dark in there you wouldn't be able to see it
Society feeds off your pain
You feed off your anger
I could be rich
But my soul would still be poor
Smile at your illusions
Drown in your lies
Pain is your lock
You'll never find the key
You'll find the gun
Place your bet
Lay down your life
I'll fight the battle
You'll lose the war
The streets have fading memories
The shoes have walked through the stories
Minds forget
Hearts don't forgive

She thinks so many things
So many things
If I wear this will he see me?
If I put on a face will he kiss me?
If I spray this will he love me again?
She can hear him parking the car
So she meets him at the door
He's been drinking again
Maybe she should hide
She wants to try
He pushes her out of the way
She hates it when he does that
She always asks herself the same question
Why did I trap myself?
She wants to break free
But he won't even let her leave the house
He calls her a whore
But he doesn't even fuck her anymore
They used to make music
Everything is just a fading memory
His breath is heavy
It makes her nauseas
He calls her a bitch
But she's forgotten how to speak outside of her head
He tells her she's fat
But he doesn't even let her eat
He used to wine and dine her
His fist is always so hard
And she's tired of wearing black and blue
She just wants to be human again
He yells that he's hungry
He's always fucking hungry
He grabs her and yells that the food taste like shit
His fist is so hard
And she hates it when he hits her there

She's fading fast
She can't take anymore
Every night she dreams of ways to break free
Tonight she'll live one
The house of her first love turned into her first prison
If she doesn't win this fight she'll die tonight
His body on the floor is her key
Now she can breath

They tell me it's my time to lie down
My time to die
No one ever showed me
I can show you my pain
So you can feel my emotion
I got lost in the game
I can tell you my secrets
So you can see my hell
But it doesn't compare to my anger
It happened back then
But I live with it today
It's proven to be chains on my soul
Putting locks on my thoughts
I got lost in the battle
In the darkness of drugs
In the darkness of alcohol
In the darkness of your soul
Fading away
Losing sight
I forgot how to remember
Crying away my years
Smoke my last cigarette
Light my first
I got lost in the world
I found pain in the village
Death in the city
Buried by their hate
I got lost in myself
My soul broken
My heart black
My mind poisoned
Out in the cold
Out in the rain
I got fucked
In your arms

I've been hiding
Hiding from your anger
Hiding from your kiss
By the streets
With my gun
My wings are broken
But I can still run

Let the door close
Let the tears flow
No more pain
No more suffering
Into the shadows
Close your eyes
It won't be long
Your time has come
My sorrow has been washed away
No my pain comes your way
My dreams of death are filled with your face
I can taste your weakness
Smell your fears
Consuming your tears
Makes my stomach ache
I miss my years
Blood for sorrow
Pain for fun
Life without choices
Love with boys
Sex with toys
Unforgiving words
Unforgiving actions
From a gentle hand to a brutal fist
Taking away life's gift
Black and blue
It's time to pay your dues
I won't take anymore
I'm not your whore
Give me my strength
Give me my pride
I'm done with you
You're not as strong as you think you are

I lock myself in chains
They provide comfort
Strange how we don't let go of the bad
Sing another song
Rack another line
Another optical illusion
Another lie
Sell me another high
They say I'm jaded
But who's to blame
My heart is torn
My soul set aflame
Sing another song
Rack another line
Another optical illusion
Another lie
Sell me another high
Tears of sorrow to highlight the pain
So fuck the world I'm going insane
I don't want to sing another song
Fuck another line
Screw optical illusions
And all the lies
Shut up and let me enjoy my high

Nichole Haggerty

I don't want you to see me
I don't want you to hear me
I don't want you to hurt me
I want to leave
I want to live
Live in your death
I want to be your untouched
I want to be everything that you won't let me
Why can't you see that you're killing me?

Your tears are your prison
Your cries are your company
Does it feel good?
Do you like it like that?
Cut yourself
Who cares if you're alone?
You don't mean anything to anyone
No one even knows you exist
Besides you can't lie to yourself
You like the blood
Your scars are your prizes
All with their own story
Stories you keep to yourself
How do you do it?
Live with so much anger
The anger that keeps you numb
It's not that you really like the pain
You just can't feel it
Your cuts become your only relief
From society, from life

In my desperate hour
I hate this life but still it goes on
The light you show is blinding
Impossible to see
The road of evil catches up to me
Stops the will to think
The will to go on
Life wrapped around me like a sad sirens song
In my desperate hour
You were never there when your help was needed
I asked so nicely begged and pleaded
Your harsh words and stone cold eyes made it easier for me to
say my goodbyes
In my desperate hour
Everything becomes a blur
Nothing makes sense anymore
Thinking becomes a useless work of the mind
My heart bleeding
My soul crying a puddle of despair
Maybe I've been sleeping all these years
Close my eyes and steal my pride
In my desperate hour
Our minds have decayed
Sorrow streaks the faces of those who know not of reality in
our hell we must stay
Our crimes we have committed now its time to pay
In my desperate hour
I'm tired of this war
I don't want to dance anymore
I would cry but my tears are running dry
In my desperate hour
Its time for me to say my goodbyes

My hope has turned into a tight rope
Thank you
I was used to the pain
Thank you
Keep your eyes closed and the bottle open
Why are you scared of your face?
All I ever wanted was your promises
All I ever got was your lies
All I wanted was to feel your touch
All I ever felt was your fist
I wanted to hear your sweet talk
All I ever heard were your convictions
I wanted to see your face
All I ever saw was your anger
All I wanted was you
All I got was your shadow

It's about pleasure
It's about pain
It's all the things that make us human
It's all the things that deny us passage
Drugs to fly
Love to kill
Blood to live
And lies that make us real
It's about fantasy
It's about fiction
Obsession to breathe
Envy to kneel
Vanity to steal
It's about loneliness
It's about comfort
It's all the things that make us feel

Where are you taking me?
Take this blindfold off my eyes
All I smell is death
All I feel is hatred
He pins me against the wall
Tears off my clothes
I feel the blade against my skin
I can smell the blood
My heart is racing
My mind won't stop spinning
He places a cup against my lips and tells me to drink
It's my own blood
My head becomes weightless
I can't hear anything
I can feel him though
Feel him inside of me
His thrust is hard, making me bleed
Which increases his anger
I want to cry out
Only my cries are whimpers
He hits me
He won't stop hitting me
Somebody please make him stop
I can feel the blade pierce my skin
I can hear my blood fall to the floor
If only he would let me go
I would never tell
Nobody would ever have to know
Please not there
I can feel the blade inside of me
He turns the knife
Please let me die
I can't take anymore
But my fear won't let my soul go
Where is he taking me?
And with a kiss he throws me into the river

I have scars on the outside
It makes you wonder how many I have on the inside
My convictions stab
My thoughts rape
I wear a smile of pain
Every tear has a story
Every story has a dragon to protect it
A wise man said hello
He told me to take off my crown of apathy
He told me to set myself free
I asked how
He told me to bleed
He told me to cry
He told me to feel
I want to bleed
The blind man holds visions that draw me in
Life is a love song
Inspired by lust
A melody of loneliness
A voice of drugs
Instruments of fear
Played by pain
It's all the things that make us human
Lies that make us real

I wasn't born to put up with your shit
Yet here I am
You tell me I can leave
But you yell that I have to stay
Can I cry for you?
Can I feel for you?
Can I kill you?
I'll change my laugh
I'll change my mind
I'll change my clothes
I'm not giving up
I'm giving in
I've had enough
You're always here
Why won't you go?
Your blood is cold
Your mind is rotten
I can see you
The man in the mirror
You're always there
I can feel you
I cry for you
Why can't I kill you?
What do you want?
Your eyes have an empty stare
Your arms hold nothing
Your arms hold strong
I can see your blood
Flow from your chest
Flow from your wrist
You're a beautiful beast
A beautiful man
You're tears flow from hollow eyes
Why can't I kill you?

Nichole Haggerty

Tears flowing from the ones who loved him
The ones who cared
Mournful faces and black clothing show our grief our loss
Yet each of us know that we truly never lost anything
For he will remain with us in our hearts and minds
Memories of times filled with laughter and loving words
An impact he put on us that no one will forget
A great man gone, but yet still here
Even though our hearts ache and our faces are streaked with sorrow
We must respect that he too
Such a great man needed his time to rest

Sometimes my thoughts overwhelm me and I just want to break down
Sometimes life runs faster than I do
Sometimes I feel like I can't go on
But then I remember when all is said and done life still goes on

Don't tell me not to be scared when I can hear your yelling in my tears
Don't tell me not to hide when I can feel your anger in my bruises
I tried to stand up but you pushed me back down
I tried to run but you caught up
I tried yelling but society was deaf
I tried so much but got so little

I could hear her screams every night
I always knew what he did to her wasn't right
His fist was hard
I always thought that it wasn't my fight
Black and blue were her colors
That night was the worst
That night was his final outburst
In the morning the ground was covered with black snow
This time I didn't turn away
On this morning I held my head low
That day my mind drowned in ignorance

Its too late, I've already been exposed
It's not the first
It's not the last
Go ahead and turn your head
Not before you steal a look
Can you see the pain?
Of course not
Everyone is blind
No one ever sees the pain
My eyes are hollow
Like my heart
I've been exposed
No one wants to stare
Although they'll take a look
Everyone wants the outside and between the thighs
They forget about the inside
My soul is bleeding tears
Although I already know on one cares

Insanity shows its face
Silence screams
Broken glass
Shattered dreams
Fading streets
Blood spilt on angel wings
Twisted faces from the shadows
Lost in thoughts
Drowning in anger
Forever goodbyes
No more hellos
It's all the same ride

Society is finding its way in
Little girls in mini skirts
Little boys with death in their hands
It's all insanity
A melting pot boiling over
Another monkey disappears
Another elephant forgets
Your questions can be answered at the bottom of another bottle
Your life can be found in your nose
A melting pot boiling over
Another monkey disappears
Another elephant forgets
Acid rain burns through another umbrella
Eyes full of color
Blind to the streets
It's all insanity
A melting pot boiling over
Another monkey disappears
Another elephant forgets
Misled minds
Unheard hearts
Life without meaning
Death without cause
Society is finding its way in

You're just an impossible princess
Another day in your world
And I'll surely die
Life's little secrets
A crow's lie
Twisted thoughts
Dark minds
Shadows rise
Lives fall
It's just another fairy tale

Can you feel it?
It's taking me over
Poisoning my thoughts
Losing control
Insanity that won't stop
I don't belong
And you don't care
Going on this way
Reassure my death
Living is not the way
Left with no meaning
Tears that won't stop flowing
If I could just make it all go away
Maybe I would be okay

My anger for you rises
With every morning sun
In the darkness I may be blind
But in the light I can see
Your skeptical illusions of life
Please my obscure mind and arouse my hatred
My dreams of death are filled with your face
I can taste your weakness
And smell your fears
Drinking your tears
Makes my stomach ache
With the passion you have stolen
One day your eyes will be free to see

I can turn you upside down
I'll kill you for fun
Speak your hatred
I'll show you my pain
You have your convictions
I have my reason
I can make you cry
I can make you sing
Place your blame
Read your lines
Tormented by the heart
Sleep in your shadows
Alcohol is your excuse
Which gives me my reason
I'll let you fade away

Will it ever change?
Will people stay the same?
My life is no more
My tears are gone
I've lost my fight
Fight with life
Fight for what's right
I've had my chance
Now they tell me it's my time to lie down
My time to die
Have you heard our screams?
They are from you
Why do we live this way?
We do what is shown
You were there to show us
Now it's our fault
That we're here

I had a friend
It was always just the two of us
But they lied to me
We stayed up late
Played on the swings
We talked about everything, we talked about nothing
I had a friend
It was always the two of us
We were outcast together
We dreamed about the world
We we're going to take the world by surprise
Prove them wrong
I had a friend
One day she wasn't there and with many more
I wondered what happened
I wondered where my friend was
Why she wasn't there
When my questions were followed by answers
I knew she was in a better place
But who was going to help take the world by surprise with me?
I had a friend
It was always the two of us
They told me the truth and now it's just me
But I'll prove them wrong for us

The night overflows the streets
Shadows rise from the dark
Violence takes on life
Actions that scream
Where are our hero's?
Where are our knights?
Living in fear
Anger becomes our strength
Someone turn on the light
Who started this fight?
Will we ever learn?
Do we have time?
Time to make things right

So many thoughts
So many emotions
I can't keep them under control any longer
I'm bursting at the seems
Answer my questions
Turn and walk away
Is there no other way?
What the fuck is going on
Is this growing up?
If so I want to go back
I'm so tired but I can't sleep
Answer my questions
Turn and walk away
Is there no other way?
What's my dream?
What's my reality?
Am I here?
I'm losing my will to go
So answer my fucking questions
Turn and walk away
There is no other way

A mix of emotions
Knowing only confusion
When will everything make sense?
When will wrong turn to right?
Always in the dark
Someone please turn on the light
Dry my eyes
Pick up my heart
Open the door and turn away
One day I'll know
Eventually I will gain sight
Maybe then things will be right

I just wanted to say thank you
Thank you for picking up the pieces
The pieces of my heart
The pieces of my mind
The pieces of my soul
Thank you for putting the pieces back together
For holding my hand
For never losing faith
I just wanted to say sorry
Sorry for my blindness
Sorry for being stubborn
I just wanted to let you know you're my angel
Through the rough waters you were my raft
When things were out of reach you became my wings
When the road got rough you gave me strength
When tears streaked my face your were there to dry them
Through the good and bad you were there
You are my angel and I just wanted to say I love you

I was scared of it all but you didn't care
I had more anger and fear in me than you'll ever know
Even though you put it there
You locked me in those chains
What did you expect?
Of course my wrists would begin to hurt
To break free I would have to break you

Maybe we are here but do we know for sure
Sometimes it feels as though the world has swallowed me whole
The light never seems to stay lit
They say reach for the sky
But never the stars
Would that be too much?
Everyone has another side
An action without a reaction
Like crying with no tears
It can be done
Only if you can see past the mirror
On to the other side

Spring turns to summer
Like I turn to you for warmth that I never find
Summer turns to fall
Like you make me do when you leave my side
Fall turns to winter
Like I freeze in your cold eyes
Winter turns to spring
Like how I look to you for something that's not true

Nichole Haggerty

To be found passionate and left lifeless
Like a bag in the wind with no soul
We walk through this unforgiving life
With tears of sorrow and pain in our hearts
Revenge in our thoughts
Pray our children never feel the same
Together we can put an end to it this time

Like a shooting star I fell
Angels without wings
Singers without voices
Artists without paintings
I've been spent
No more tears
Life with only useless years
Just another scar
Written off on the wall
I'll drown in my sorrows
I'll remember the pain
Only to pretend that I forgot
I'll tie a bow around my neck
Put myself back on the shelf
Maybe I might just sell
Wishful thinking
Thoughts too big for the mind
Insanity holds the power
I hold the key
Unlock the door
Walk in with blind eyes
Vanity in my face
Naïve, young and dumb
That's all I am to them
Stand on top and come out last
Taste the best
Fuck all the rest

Goodbye is forever
So we'll just say see ya
Remember if you need a laugh
I'm a phone call away
If you need a shoulder to cry on
Just remember I'm only a day away
So follow the angels until I find my way

Things are never what they seem
People never tell you what's really on their mind
Everyone lives in their own lies
So much pain that we ignore
So much violence that we all share
Love is hating
Hitting is our way of touch
A race so ignorant
Everyone plays the game
No one ever wins
It's our own poison
It's our prison
Chain our hands behind our back
Cover our eyes
Take your last step
It's your time die

Let me be free
Break away from this pain
I know you want me
But I can't even breathe
I know you care
But I don't even care about me
My chains have no key
My mind doesn't shut off
Memories don't fade away
A broken heart can last forever
Your shit may not stink
But mine does
I can't even love myself
So what makes you think I can love you?

You were born with no innocence
You oppress the free mind
With manipulation and greed
You rob the lovers of their passion
I can see your scars of life
I can hear your screams of death
You taunt the knife with only a taste of skin
And paralyze the use of words

My price is high
You'll pay in tears
Society has cast you away
Prosecution without defense
Don't be scared
They'll smell your fear
The unlived life is the life of envy
Your pain is high
Your tolerance is low
This is a fight you won't win
This will leave scars if you give in

She drinks milk from a wine glass
She cries alone in the light
Sings in the darkness
A life with bars
A passion with wings
And hatred that burns
You'll stare in wonder
Become blind to the pain
It's this way because that's your choice
You'll let our children die
And watch the streets cry

Trying to pass time
Watching TV
Reading books
Writing down your thoughts
Thoughts you don't want to remember anyway
You cut your hair and change the color
Underneath you're still the same
You cry to feel better but it makes you feel worse
You listen to songs that stab your heart
And make memories flash by so fast that you feel nauseas
This isn't what you grew up to be
It's who you have become

They're our soldiers
That day was different
That day our dad came home
He was still in uniform
My brother was still a baby
Unsure of the figure in the door
My mom cried
My sister was excited
I realized how expensive freedom is
They're our soldiers
My father
Your son
They're our soldiers
Your husband
My brother
They're our soldiers
Your wife
Your sister
They're our soldiers
Our family
In everyway
We'll tie a yellow ribbon
Pray every night
In our hearts we'll keep them
Until they find they their way

I have secrets that I can never share
No ones intangible
And I'm far from righteous
These secrets
They keep me alive
They're my truth
My sacrifices are my choice
They give me a reason to bleed
A reason to cry
No ones intangible
And I'm far from righteous
You stole what was mine
Things that you can never give back
Your words lock my hands
Make me buckle in the knees
I wish I could make you bleed
Cry damn it cry
For all that you took from me
No ones intangible
And I'm far from righteous

It was like any other morning
She is tall, slender and beautiful in everyway
Her story has no ending and always the same beginning
Her addiction to cocaine keeps her alive
In another way
This morning she found herself covered in blood
Lying on the kitchen floor
Another failed attempt
It took a minute for eyes to focus
To stop her head from spinning
She stood up and that was enough to bring up the evening before
She grabbed a sponge
Trying to clean up all the evidence
She didn't need to think about last night
She would never remember anyway
Her kitchen smelt like a cleaning solution
She went to the bathroom to wash away the pain
She wondered how much more she could take
Although already knowing that this was the end

How strong are you
When you run
How brave are you
When you hide
Kneel to the ground
Pray to the sky
Salvation keeps you alive
Even after you die
How fierce are you
When you fight
How much can you take?
The war may be over
The battle has not yet been fought
Will you be ready?
Will you be willing?
When the light is shown
Can you believe in only what your eyes see?
It may be too late
Damnation may already have you

The sounds get louder
The mind grows weaker
Pain shoots through more than the heart
I'm always wrong
You're the one that taught me
How can you be scared?
When you're the one that showed me fear
Loneliness brings new hopes
Frustrations breed anger
Too many reasons to hold onto the past
Never enough to move forward
Will this ever change?
Will my memories of you ever fade?

Life can be such sweet sorrow
When light drowns out the pain
The path sometimes gets narrow
Let your soul fly
Life is too short to let it pass you by
From jaded and bitter
To dragon tears

About the Author

Born in northeast Philadelphia at the age of eight she moved with her family to Germany in response to her dads job as now a master sergeant in the United States Air Force. In Germany Nichole witnessed Neo-Natzi demonstrations. Her life on a military base brought to life the movies of war. Men patrolling the base with M-16's and tanks. Bomb threats toward the school and her father leaving to fight wars in the name of freedom.

www.ingramcontent.com/pod-product-compliance
Lightning Source LLC
Chambersburg PA
CBHW020400290526
45785CB00005B/2376